BLUE

Nyamthian Tangjang

PAPER TOWNS
PUBLISHERS

PAPER TOWNS
PUBLISHERS

First published by
Papertowns Publishers
72, Vishwanath Dham Colony,
Niwaru Road, Jhotwara,
Jaipur, 302012

Blue: God even made the sky blue as if it knew

ISBN Print Book – 978-93-94670-17-4

Cover by Neha Agrawal
nehaa.2089@gmail.com

BLUE

Nyamthian Tangjang

Acknowledgement

I wish to express my gratitude to everyone who generously helped me in this new start. To the publishers, who gave their expertise, assurance, and helped me color my first official book and for opening a door.

To my family and friends for giving me my memories. My mother for believing in me and convincing my father. My sister, thank you for always being with me and my loving brothers for understanding me.

To my lovely friends for the support and for the laughs, thanks Mamtu, for pushing me to try and not give up.

And my dear readers, who are willing to give me a chance by picking up this book.

Thanks to all of you.

Dedication

Dedicated to Avi with love. (My Late Grandmother)

don't tell me
It is not possible
It is just a dream
because I am a dreamer
I dream of a life
and I am a dreamer
and if I don't dream
I do not have a life

IMPERFECTION IS BEAUTY

WE ALL ARE IMPERFECT

Open your heart
do not be afraid of sorrow
as it leads us
to the way
of
happiness.

A bitter truth was
hidden behind a face
nobody wants to look at.

Looking out the window
what do you see?
Even the air has
changed its color,
the clouds have become moody.
As just now the sky was bright,
and now it's raining.

There are certain things
that I want
from me
for me.

Kindness,
patience,
and love

Shower with love every morning.
Eat with patience.
And live with kindness.

You were told
you've to do more
to be more like them
so you work
day and night
and cut the pieces
that you adore.

It hurts badly, so you told them
"I wish to be just the way I am"
They said
"you are not in the position to raise your voice, little darling"
and they sealed your lips
just so no one can hear your
cries.

I was running with no shoes on
while it was raining.
I looked back to see
from whom I was running away;
there were shadows following me,
trying to engulf me in.
I fell on my face and
woke up on my bed.
I took a breath of relief.
But was that really a dream?

No matter
how damn hard
you try.
You cannot hate
if you do not love.

At first
I was beautiful,
then childish,
and lastly
I was intolerable.
But it was
just
you
changing your mind.

Long time ago
I wished for a thing
and waited for it to happen.
Decades have passed
the due date has expired
now it is just a wishful thinking.
I still force my mind
to remember those days
when I used to believed that
shooting stars can get me things.
How simple and naïve was I.
That innocence,
I wish for you again.

Tell me a name of a liar
who can lie better than me.
The lies I tell everyone
about who I am
are so believable that
sometimes I see a
stranger in the mirror
laughing at me.

I was in a dilemma
I did not notice
when I started wearing
a darker shade of blue.

I was raised with love.
But the competition overshadowed it.
I was running at a race
where only the top were certified.
hence came the feeling of worthlessness.
I am good at other games,
I tell myself.
Yet, being pushed to the
same race again
I fall.

Inked myself in the back
of my shoulder,
chose the word in a
foreign language.

I draw it beautifully.

People did not understand
the meaning and I enjoyed it.
It was so simple;
it shows out loud "rare".

My eyes are swollen
from our last night's fight.
Said pretty much everything,
I never had.
We were in some
kind
of situation,
playing who hurts whom the most.
The match got drawn,
one of us had to step back
but I don't think
it is now.

You think
you know the reason behind
those sketches on my body.

I will tell you,
they are called
the art of lies.

If I am trapped inside my body,
then how am I supposed to fly?

----------faces

It was surreal,
her hospitality towards everyone
made me believe that
she was more than kind.

Then I saw another face of hers.
Mean, dominating, and rude.
That could kill thousands
just with words.

When I finally decided,
I understood her.
I found her crying,
broken, and in vain.

Then she got up,
picked her pieces;
and stood strong.

I realized,
she had many faces.
A different face to face a different face.

Sometimes all you need is a lie;

Just to keep you alive.

I fed
you all
of my
emotions
and now
I am
broke.

My mother painted my body
with some shades of brown,
gave me the intelligence
to speak with my mouth.

My father shared his
narrow eyes,
so do not tell me
I cannot see lies.

I have a little nose
and I can smell a culprit.

I walk with the height
of the mountains,
where I was born;
and lead my brothers and sisters
to make every place
we visit
our home.

I believe in believe.
So I will wait and wait.
These agonies,
I will use you as my rhythm
to sing in front of
the live stage.

Recently started taking poison,
a little drop everyday
mixed with my tea.
Getting loud and unclear
the side effects are seen.

But I hope the day will come
when a snake bite
won't kill me.
Instead,
I will watch it die.

Nothing lasts forever,
it is said in a book.

Learn the word endure;
so I enjoy the pain.

Because if the day is glooming;
the night will have stars.

Where the Sun and the moon;
meet in secret;
I will have my dance.

Opportunities came but I had to blow.
I was so disappointed and didn't
want to accept the truth.
Many were happy and some were shocked.
The decision I made was hard,
to say it in a sentence;
it was unacceptable.
I question everyone's intelligence.
But why I am the one,
who is hurting the most.
When everything I did was for a selfish reason.

Oh dear, you should stop asking to a closed door.

I have gained a few weights on my shoulders.

You can address it as a burden.

I am now labelled as not attractive,

the tag never really compliments.

People have stopped visiting my place.

It is kind of like a deserted home now.

Recklessly invited some unknown faces,
they came with their fake identities.
I said 'it is okay' to myself;
go dance away the pain
it is just for a night.
But forgot that
tomorrow are endless.

Episodes of trauma started playing,
when I had a glimpse of you
at the crowd.
And you were never really there.

Destiny is twisting my world upside down,
or maybe I am walking in a wrong path.
So it is trying to fix me up
by breaking me down.

Your single touch was enough to
break down my walls
and ruin me.

In love

I caught you smiling to yourself one day.
It leads me to wonder what were you smiling at
Or
Who is in your head?
And I asked you the reason.
But you were so lost in your head,
my questions never got your attention.
Maybe you had already
given it to someone else.
I looked into your eyes,
even your eyes were smiling
and they were lost, too.

Just then, I knew that you were gone.

Why do you say that I am in a different world?
I am in the same world as you,
I am just keeping my silence.
Because I am busy trying to figure out,
what are you behind those covers of yours.
Are you hiding some deep secrets,
but from who and why are you hiding those.
I am listening to all of your actions.
I am reading your style.
So again I asked,
Why do you say that I am in a different world
when I am in that same world,
as you.

sorry was so precious for me
that I waited long enough
even though I was losing myself
and by the time it came
it was so late that
I was nowhere to be found.

The fragrance you thought you gave,
was a pungent smell
which is over forever
so, goodbye, now.

I don't know
my brain does not believe my eyes
and my eyes cannot understand
whatever my brain says
or is it just me?

Love was the gift that I received from you,
and shared with everyone else but you.
I was just cruel.

Runaway to a place
where no one knows me
the idea is enough
to keep me awake at nights.

A place where you
don't carry the
bag of expectations
and any failure.

Where there are no limits for happiness.

Is it possible or am I asking for too much?

Living in curse.
So I am breathing
hate.

I am really sorry
If I ever made you feel
like you were nothing.
I know I never say things
that are needed for both of us
I know I do not go with you
I keep my mind and
my everything with only me.
I also know that
that is what is keeping us apart.
But I am just too afraid
to even speak a word.

What if you were a wolf
dressed in a sheep's clothing?

I have a hobby,
my new pass time
the habit to
torture me and
my loved ones.

Tell me what is worse than getting
stabbed by the ones you thought
were yours.
Tell me how to love yourself
when you get bathed in fire.
Be strong, be strong
believe yourself
are just words now.
When the ones
who gave you
those words
are the ones
that make
you weak.

I did whatever I was told
just to please the unknown
I was working in other's control.
When I said I am also human,
I was isolated and locked away
in a dark room.
Don't know how many days later
they came and said something
and like a machine
I followed.

What a waste of time to think
about the times you can't have back.
Yet, here you are showing anguished cries,
wishing if only you acted differently and
everything would have been alright.

Her smile
she thought a curse
everything she touched
turned into dust.

Easy is to believe the wrong
try the hard part,
erase the wrong.

Free

The villain of my story was breathing right beneath me,
wearing the smile of a protector.
With a cloth tied in my eyes
I followed every instruction
to get into the dirt water.
Now I speak like it,
I act like it;
but I never intended
to become like it.
My reflection changed.
My shadow disappeared.
What have I done?
When I ask,
why can't I do what I love to do?
It said "WHY? Because I said so, that's why."
It made me want to be reborn again.
So it was decided;
I went to the cliff
I looked down and saw the claiming water
calling my name.

I was ready to lose it all,
and to have it all
in the next life.
Just then a little birdy sat
on my shoulder
and sang;
you had sown and now you will reap
the happiness is within you
do not look for it.
Instead, seek in your soul
set yourself free
you are all you need.

We lie
We pretend
We do things that are forbidden
We break hearts
We became rebels
You know what they say
We are born sinners.

When it hurts
You will remember me
When it will rain
You will remember the tears I shed
That I thought were for you
When in real it was for me
As I had to forget to remember you.

Dear almighty Mother,
Thank you for everything.
For protecting us, our family
And, also for guiding us.
Oh, greatest giver
Thank you for the strength
And the power
And for helping us to be
Kind and understanding
So that we can stay close
by heart and forever.

The saddest thing was,
I could not fight myself.

Woke up feeling heavy,
washed my face
looked for my reflection
found empty
I saw nobody
so, when did I lose myself?

__________reality the worst gift ever received

She had you at your worst,
but you gave your worst at your best.

Blinded by the lie
that makes us satisfy
is the truth that we
don't see for a thousand times.

But no matter how many times
you run away from it.
It will come to you
finding its way back.

So better face and fight
without fearing the consequences
or else it will
haunt you for life.

Just like the different colors in a rainbow,
you taught me different ways of being strong.

Words were not enough
actions were not enough
it had ruined so deep that
affection was scared
to show itself
as it may take it
in a wrong way.

It is all about the period of time,
one day it will heal
and the scars will be
beautiful to look at.

PRACTICE

You said that practice makes them perfect
It is all a part of a lie
Beautiful, well-presented lie
For the eyes.

OBSERVER

You were a keen observer
And I believed every word
Of yours and thought
You were magical.

I gave you all I had,
everything I had earned.

At the end
when it was over
you were gone and
I saw the truth.

TRICKED

I had been tricked
by you, a con artist
in this carnival
name relationship.

Where you robbed everything
and left me empty handed.

The weather is wry
winter's early this time.
I prepared a hot bath for myself
with scented candles and rose petals to compliment
and salt and bubbles for healing.
As soon as I dipped in
the fragrance washed my dirt
and my body soaked all the joy.
Because this time I will keep myself warm
Even in the heavy rainfall.

I promise my inner self
we are strong and we will go on.

I am pouring it all out today.
I loved you and I don't hate you
anymore.

What if reality was only a dream?
Shall we pretend like our eyes were closed
because there would be no more regrets?
Or should I be sad for the loss of all my memories
that I had made.
All the things I had learned from my mistakes
will be taken away from me and
I might do the same old things again.
And call it a deja-vu of some kind.

My personality, I was quiet.
I gave people the luxury
of assumptions.
The misunderstanding, they are
easy and the cause of my mental breakdown.
It made me stuck there forever.
What is happy? I stopped feeling.
But I love me and to prove it
I had to recite the story
"there's a life behind those walls".

If you are waiting for that one day
then stop, it will never come.
If you are afraid to cry out
let it all out or you might
breakdown at the wrong time.

Wise are those who read the signs well.
Their impact speaks depth,
what they want
they do.
There's nothing like, I give up.
Foolish are the lot
confuse between love and lie.
And then come the cowards,
trying hard to believe in something
vague and not so genuine.

Do what your heart implies.

Keep your smile even when you die inside.
Make a conversation even if the person
is someone you do not want to know.
Live just like the way it was suggested.
Do certain things pretending like you are someone else.
Doing what grown-ups are supposed to do.

There was a sea of emotions running down
yesterday when I suddenly woke up at 3:33am.
I was so accurate, I was shocked.
Where did they come from?
What where they?
What do they want from me?
Was I supposed to invite?
I was in the midst of my thoughts
that I did not notice,
it ran out.

Someone told me I was bad with words,
I started writing.
I wrote a few pages
and wanted to recite.
So I went to someone else,
someone else was listening
but failed to understand.
Well, at least they listened, I appreciated.
I wanted someone,
longing for a presence.
Never recognising I was born with it.

It was raining in the afternoon,
it enlightened the fire in me
and I started dancing to it.
I cannot resist it honestly.
It felt so good and calm,
I almost got mixed in it.
And oh yes,
it did not hurt.
Even after dancing with bare feet.

Things were unfinished between us,
at first I wanted to communicate
and say whatever was in my
heart and mind.
Thought it was necessary.
Time passes by hours, days, months and years.
Now I know, it was meant to be.
The things that I had to learn, understand
and to let go.
It was all meant to be.

My words are precious.
And I must not waste it,
on just anybody.

Moved my house to a new location.
I was thinking about mountains
and ended up beside the river.
It took me half of the year
to complete the decoration.
Yes, longer than the expectations.
Invited all the warmth and light
that I will need in the time of darkness.
There's no limit and everyone came along.
So thrilled to see the water, they all swam.
My purpose, I recognized and announced,
first I will learn to swim and then
shift my home to the mountains
to climb.

How many hours do you sleep?
It doesn't matter,
I don't dream.

Don't be afraid to be an outcast,
a person who is rejected from the society.
If you don't fit in with them,
change your direction and seek for your true self.
Everyone has someone waiting for them.
We will find them.

Let us not hurry and take our time.
As it takes a long time to build a home
with the outcome so beautiful and so strong.
Let our foundation be pure and our boundaries full of plants.
Just so when the hate passes through them,
it turns them into fresh love.
As it comes from a place that's true, warm and fragile.
As together we are
in the garden of paradise.

Legend said
Many have different stories
with one same character.
The one bad guy
who tempts you to have a taste
from the fountain of youth.

It is up to the person
who is under the temptation.
God has made everyone with equal love.
While only some chose to starve
and many others;
many others fall into the dark water.

She has the same gaze as mine
sad and doubtful,
but why does it make me feel good.
Knowing she is going through pain.
Am I evil or am I the hate?
Or is it because
now I have a companion
who can understand.

The stares I gather when
I walk into the room
I don't think they are nice.

Some tell me to go back,
and some have laughing eyes.

I try to ignore the intimidation,
but it feels like I am walking
the walk of shame.

Because I am in the middle of the circle
and now there's no going back.

Do not judge me by the colors I show
I have every season in me
I change.
Some days
I paint the sky black,
Some days
I dance with the rain.
I am like a secret diary
hard to find but
easy to read.
And if you keep me real close,
I will be your healer.
The one that
you will
always
need.

When I was a child,
I used to chase the moon
and believed it was
following me.

Counting stars
was pure joy,
and not
just a hobby.

A priceless position
you cannot deal with diamonds.
My sister, my wise man,
my brother, my soldiers,
and my parents, my guardians.
I am loved by the one's I love.
This is my realm.

She was born a prey
yes, that is what they say,
be quite unless you
want to get trapped.

She was trained inside
the cage and was never
allowed to test her limits.
She was always under arrest.

Once a while she got a permit
to breath in a peaceful environment.

But when she went out she wore
the dullest expression.

They told her to be
thankful for the cage.
There are hunters out there,
their eyes are everywhere.

But she was excited and forgets the risk.
The glitters inside her were now everywhere.

Like a blissful soul she flies up high.
And forgets that she was tired.

Did not notice that the night came,
and it was time to go back home.
But before that she was thirsty
so she went down towards the pond.

When she bent to drink,
she saw a devil behind;
ready to capture her in.

Like an instinct she flies away.
But could hear the devil say;
There are plenty of me
let's see how long you'll
survive.

Cruel behavior ran in your blood
Act of offence to any kind of love
Rude was the first word
I heard coming out of your mouth
To change your attitude
Became my strong desire
Because there's so much love
I wish you could see
So I made up my mind
to teach you believe
But to become like the one
with the curse was the only cure

And that is how I bet my life to make yours.

I am afraid of the feelings
that do not have a name,
they come and go as if
they live in my home
without paying any rent.

Something so mysterious and
haunting is the only thing
I know about it.
And when I chased them away;
they enter from a different exit.

In love I had lost and in love I will find again all the things I once had.

I have to win it back.

Let me be your inspiration.
Paint me on your walls
in red, blue, green and purple.
Dream about me.
Let me be the only one,
your heart desires.

I like the way you look at me and listen to me.
It was like; you saw something in me that I was not able to see.
So I acted like I did not notice when you took pictures of me.
Just so I can keep those moments as my souvenir.

She ran into her arms and
cried until she fell sleep.
But even in her dreams;
she panics.

I am the cause of it.

It was all because of me.

I let it start and encourage it.

Now I have to put the fire out even if I burn myself.

_______my oath

I refuse to be a victim of your abuse.
Those days are gone and your fashion is old.
There is a difference between raising your voice and being loud.
You were raised loud but I learnt to listen before I open my mouth.

I listen so I can understand,
I understand that I have a voice;
so I am now speaking the truth.

I have everything that I need.
I am capable of helping myself.
When I am weak, I am strong.
If I am tired, I rest and never stop.

I can do anything and everything,
with time and practice.
The dedication is in my soul.

I am my father.
I am my mother.
I can take care of myself.

There is so much hate inside me,
that I am blind now.
I don't accept your kind gesture,
I always refuse.
I try to be free but;
I have my doubts.
So I have to tell you,
it is not about you
it is about me.
I am the bad guy now.

A famous scene from a drama was playing;
lovers were tested for their faith.
The one whom she trusted the most
turned out to be the devil
disguised in an angel's face.

I let you walk on my flower carpet,
you came with the foul odor.
I made you my best food,
you flipped your plate and
let it go to waste.
I wore my flawless gown
with beautiful design in it,
just so I can impress you.
But you saw what you wanted to believe,
I was unpleasant even after everything I did.

Make a group against me.
It is useless,
I have no fear left in me.
Talk rubbish about me,
they cannot travel far
to reach my ears.
Lay your best plan for me.
Trap me or kill me.
Even if I fall into your plot,
I will rise against your pity game.
I will proselyte.
Oh, you don't realize that
you bring me my true revival.

In the midst of my thoughts,
I saw some blurry shadows
luring me in,
in the deep.
The blind guides,
I followed.

If I had known that
there will be a war of rumors,
I would have kept my
door locked.

But I got swayed by
your appearances,
and let you
sleep on my cot.

Ever since you came,
I am a junk
not your equal.
So why are you here in this place?
You should go back
to your palace
where you,
the majesty,
you are always right .

Don't stay and say
that the food tasted bad,
when I served you
the only bread that I had.

Don't come with your foggy aura
and say I am not touchable,
just to push me on a
journey of tribulation.

You open your mouth and did not say a word.

You got my curiosity.

I like your silence.

Oh, weak with a small mouth,
the words coming out of you
are a little and a lot loud.

The rage that you poured on me,
and enjoyed to watch me burn
until I turned into ashes.

But the city that you live in;
is full of your debts.
The weight, one day
it might collapse.

______anxiety

My mind says;
think about all the wrong decisions
you had made in the past.
I listen to her and tortured myself.

My heart says;
don't be afraid to trust me,
I promise it won't hurt.
I listen to her and hurt myself.

Every day I wake up
and struggle to fight myself.
As she is the one who wants
to kill herself.

I saw you from a distance,
and lost myself in awe.
I travelled far to get close to you.
And now I am covered with blemishes all around.

Out of envy ;
I chose to stay
as close as I can with you.
Your harsh attitude towards me,
I taught myself to exclude.
You kicked me out but
I kept my place.

Instead I should have been long gone,
before the sun went to rest.

But like a foolish fool
I made myself believe
that I can change
your ravage.

You utter curses
with flow of a waterfall,
that knows there's no comeback
from the down river.
And forget that I have
a heart that absorbs all
the harshness when you
shower me with your anger.
I know I am known for forgiveness,
but this is the last time
I am ignoring your
blaspheme.

Taking it slow
finally this time
enjoying all of the blarney.

I am falling in love
with my new appearances.
My reflection,
I earned my true identity.

Dear beauty,
I find you there
wherever I go,
holding a placard
waiting for me.

You can visit me sometimes,
I will welcome you anytime.
I want to return the pleasure,
and show my sincerity.
My dear beauty.

Most important things in life
were always by my side.
But
like a color blind
I was unable to define.

Somewhere far from close
but not out of reach,
you force out all the
love inside of me.
I was hiding because
I was waiting for
the perfect timing.
When the perfect timing
is right here,
when we live.

My head is full of good contents.
The chapters include
the sacrifices for the better conclusion.
It is not me speaking;
but the person that has
risen against the birth pain.

I used to sketch,
because I thought
I did not have the
ability to color.

But after the storm
passed away;
I finally began
to paint.

Writing a love letter and
hiding it deep inside of me,
in a secret place where
only I can find and read.

But in an accident,
if you find and understand;
the writing written
in codes.

Then consider yourself
the lucky one.
You will know that,
I am gold.

Fall with a purpose,
just to see your actual concern.

You started to laugh,
showed no hesitation
but got trapped.

I was the bait,
and now you my prisoner.

How do you feel
when you are alone
or are you even alone
or do you even feel
are your emotions numb
by your harsh encounters
I am sure there's plenty of regrets
everyone has made
certain decisions
without giving a proper thinking
consequences
they wiped
but if you enjoy
being alone in the desert
then you have to die
and be reborn again.
this beautiful world
cannot be a waste

Why do you call it a sincere
apology and the next thing
you do is the exact same thing
you drag
you isolate
and make me wait
when all I ever ask from you
was a proper goodbye

I laid down in the middle
of the highway at midnight,
and saw the distance
between far and close.

I remember everything
even the little details.
I remind myself to be afraid
but it failed to reach.

I am fearless so
when tomorrow comes
I will walk again with many
strangers on the same road.

Where I left my foot prints,
but no one can see;
only I have the privilege.

I will devote myself with all of me;
you just have to let me love you.

Having a little break from the chaos I had made,
sweeping away all the dust.

________-jealousy

I am happy for you.
And a little upset for myself.
You got what I could not have.

I swear I prayed for you,
to have everything on your plate.
But still I also wished for the same.

Wednesday night was long.
My eyes, I can't close.
I was dreaming,
a nightmare.

The curtains fall,
and the show's on,
playing the song
the dark paradise.

People from mystic kingdom had arrived.
They came with magical presents.

Every one of us has received our gifts,
written in cursive.

But they long for the ones
that do not belong to
their name.
It's classic.

People will say;
she's such a fool,
she gave up the things
that she could have.

But I rather say;
I made a great decision.
The choice I made
to choose always my happiness.

Always have the power to perform
the speech of different emotions
at every different occasion.

Always have the courage to
show the different sides
of your moods.

As always being able to show
how you feel is called bravery.
We don't have to worry.

End of December is near,
but the time stands
still between us.

The fine line,
I wish you to cross
and reach out for me.

I am dying to step out
of these rents and
search for my place.

Just like the birds,
I want to migrate
but never come back.

Not much has changed.
I can still see none.
I will go away.

But the time stands
still between us,
and you say that the
end of December is near.

At the moment of examination
my members stood against me,
my soul was divided into pieces.
I was not able to stand.
The thorny path grew taller
and choked me to death.
The rocky road,
I could not survive.

I am mixed with the sand.
No plant no flowers;
it's always a fruitless harvest.

Take and leave,
the things you did
are hard to forgive.
Do not dare to compare
yourself to my ideal.
The heart that you broke,
has turned black and cold.
You don’t need to knock.
It's a hard concrete wall.

Out of nowhere you contacted me
with your apologies for your old flaws.
And demanded me to give you back
the old me that was yours.
When from the very beginning;
I was never really yours.

I want to laugh
without the fear of crying
later.

A hopeless dream
wrapped in silk,
no one can bring
any harm to it.

With eyes open,
I am living the theme
a peaceful life in my
enchanted kingdom.

Here harmony is served every day.
So starvation is merely a cause.
People celebrate each other,
spreading love everywhere.

Ran out of words;
you left me speechless.
You asked me 'what have you ever done for me'?
How can I answer that?
When I thought you knew everything that I had gone through for you.
I gave you what I had.
Argued with people who said you were not enough.
I fought for the last flower to give it to you.
And you told me that I was never your guide.
I experienced the worst things just to make you aware.
Just to show you the happy path,
so you can walk without doubts and hesitation.
And now I am being questioned for my own deeds.
Why?

Overflowing with goodness,
your faith is gold.
Believe In yourself.
It is the greatest possession,
you will ever hold.

___________be kind

Everything will be done,
according to the saying.
You shall give love,
if you want to receive love.

Nothing is free and,
we are living in debt;
nothing is yours and,
nothing is mine.

Have you ever experienced a mental breakdown?
As if, you want to quit your senses but
you are too afraid to admit the crime.
You poured your frustration inside a closed room and
cried until your throat was dry.
Too scared to speak so
you started avoiding occasions.
Locked your front door
while you lie awake inside.
Have you ever been alone in a crowd?
Do you ever doubt yourself at your signature talent?
If you had ever felt like empty;
then you are not alone.
It will all pass,
and you will enter
your new life.

The written story is about to change.
All of the blurry ideas are coming to life.
Accepting the past was the first step,
Kept an open heart and mind
and I healed myself.

Forgiving me was the hard part.
But after saying yes,
the things are in line.
And after every completion,
I am marking a tick
one by one.

The stars in your eyes are missing.
The lights, they are dim too.
I hope that one day
you will find your hope again.
I promise even the bad things
always come to an end.

I felt naked.

You tore me apart;

miserably, without any mercy.

Standing with a suspicious posture;
I knew you were on something new.
I saw your feathers,
you were ready to fly.
And then someone told you
that the festival got cancelled.
It was bad timing.
But we do not believe
what others say,
and busted in
another's celebration.

Your smile compliments your features.

Wear it often.

_______weathering has an end

Never ready for a sudden
exposure
towards softness.

I weaved until I was weary.

I will definitely find a way out.

And take you with me
to a
bitter sweet feeling.

We were
in a
different
state.
Hot and cold,
When you
melted
I became harder.

I wanted to be a wax figure when
I was a child, a little girl.
My dreams were whatever was popular.
Some days that and the other days this,
my mind, like a climate
it always used to change.
My stories made my friends wearisome.
But I am thankful for the
patience they had.
My elders carried me on their
backs when I used to fall
asleep after playing a little too much.
Those little things still live
rent free in my head,
my store room, my precious collection.
And the fantasy to become a wax figure
has lost its power on the way,
my acceptance.

Forgive her for her appearance,
she holds a rich heart.
A tiny little diamond but
sharp just like a glass,
her shine can make
one and many blind.
And can cut the arms
of the darkness.
Listen clearly
to her quietness,
never misunderstood
for rudeness, as she observes.

The truth lies in your heart.
So speak, I will give you a new tongue.
You are special and you are unique.
All of us are same in our own homes.
Go out if you want to be known.

Heaven
tells me
I have a guaranteed protection.

I am
my own hero
of a great value.

It's getting late.
I should go back home.
Maybe we will see each other
tomorrow or the day after that.
Maybe in the park or at the coffee shop,
or maybe with some confidence;
I might tell you that my only
desire has always
been you.

Her life
obviously short as she donated
it to her loved ones, every other.
Her occupation,
a nature lover,
she gives flavor to the earth.

Draw a margin
between you and me.
The easiest thing you can do,
I expected it from you.
Your salty behavior,
you are muttonhead.
If you push me;
I will drag you out.
I have my limits.

Surrounded
by a committee
performing
the sacrifice of the lamb.

The void
that I had inside,
I tried many tries to fill it.
I faked and pretended and
let people misunderstood my image.
Stayed in someone else's house without
the invitation and they did not care.

So many directions
went to all wrong ones.
Hoping that you might see the bad
if I do it to myself.

So slowly blocked the entire road,
and waited for you to
come and take me away with you.
But if you take a little than more,
I am afraid I won't exist anymore.

I was once feeble- minded.
Chains of unwanted thoughts,
my usual daily invite.
Creating partitions
was a regular routine.
Wrote a sign of no entry
and hung it on my door.

But it is all in the past now,
now all the signs
are of green lights.
All my customers
are a regular delight.
And I am the host.
I organized.

Wealth of wisdom
shall be your pride.
Always follow the principle,
to never cheat to your inner self.
Let you be the most important thing
that must be dealt with first.
And when you hear cries of help,
show no anger and give other only
your pleasure.

Endure all the negative comments and
convert it into your unbreakable strength.
Engage with people who speak
the language of self-improvement.
Build an empire of emit humans
and teach from the book of grace.

Be decent
do not spoil your character
be warm to the cold and
overcompensate when guilty
be the flower in the mud bath

Deactivate your account of muteness
and build some courage to speak.
You will be heard
in the crowd of the crowd.
And everyone will stand with you.
All you need is “trust” in you,
because you have the power
for thee recreation.

My mind has started listening to my own thoughts.
My heart forgives and forgives my old self.
My mouth sings with the voice of wit.
My soul is inside my own body.
My reunion,
I am born again.

The one with the authority
speaks to me and presents me
with ideas when I am consciously unconscious.
It makes me believe in what I already have.
It tells me I was born to break the man-made laws.
As I have a fire burning in my soul.

The heart starts to ache
whenever the reminder rings
and I come to my sense,
that one day
I have to leave.
That one day
I want to delay
as long as I can
and cherish
the simplicity,
the neighborhood
where I grew up.
It will become
my refreshing memories.
My old days, they won't comeback.

And sometimes I want to refuse the reality.

________seek and you will find

I came out into the world
with a purpose, I always knew.
But when I opened my eyes,
it was hidden somewhere unknown.

As I grew I forgot and blended in.
It was as if I was dreaming a dream.
Then the time pushes me to a
place that never invites me in.

And so, sometime later
I recognized my purpose.
Change places to seek,
where I hope I might find.

So many sacrifices;
and I almost lose myself.
But now I am where I belong.
Yes, I am right here.

I was in the deep blue,
I was drowning low.
Struggled for breath
and every second was long.
Closed my eyes in defeat and
waited to set my soul free.
And right then my hands
and legs started to move.
Thus, that is how
I learnt to swim.

IMPERFECTION
IS BEAUTY.
WE ALL ARE
IMPERFECT

BLUE

GOD EVEN MADE THE SKY BLUE

AS IF IT KNEW

About the Author

Nyamthian Tangjang is the author of the book "BLUE". This is her first official poetry book. She received her bachelor of science from Rajiv Gandhi university. She is from northeast part of India, Arunachal Pradesh. She loves her family and art in all forms. She enjoys food, books and music. You can visit her Instagram page @___nyamthian

THANKYOU